T5-CVC-305

CRISISPOINTS FOR WOMEN

WHEN YOUR MARRIAGE DISAPPOINTS YOU

JANET CHESTER BLY

NAVPRESS

A MINISTRY OF THE NAVIGATORS
P.O. BOX 6000, COLORADO SPRINGS, COLORADO 80934

The Navigators is an international Christian
organization. Jesus Christ gave His followers
the Great Commission to go and make disciples
(Matthew 28:19). The aim of The Navigators is to
help fulfill that commission by multiplying laborers
for Christ in every nation.

NavPress is the publishing ministry of The Navigators. NavPress publications are tools to help
Christians grow. Although publications alone can-
not make disciples or change lives, they can help
believers learn biblical discipleship, and apply what
they learn to their lives and ministries.

© 1990 by Janet Chester Bly
All rights reserved, including translation
ISBN 08910-93281

Cover illustration by Phil Boatwright.

CRISISPOINTS FOR WOMEN series edited by
Judith Couchman.

This series offers God's hope and healing for life's
challenges.

All Scripture quotations in this publication are
from the *Holy Bible: New International Version*
(NIV). Copyright © 1973, 1978, 1984, International
Bible Society. Used by permission of Zondervan
Bible Publishers.

Printed in the United States of America

FOR A FREE CATALOG OF
NAVPRESS BOOKS & BIBLE STUDIES,
CALL TOLL FREE 1-800-366-7788 (USA)
or 1-416-499-4615 (CANADA)

C O N T E N T S

*For all the gals
who wanted to quit
but didn't!*

ACKNOWLEDGMENTS

This project would have been impossible to complete without the encouragement and assistance of my husband, Steve;

the input and guidance of a very able editor, Judith Couchman;

the support of many prayer partners, including Jentine Arkema and Linda Myles on the NavPress prayer team. ■

Do Yourself a Big Favor

*Let this study guide help
your marriage.*

When I mentioned that my husband and I
would be speaking at a couples' conference,
the hotel clerk leaned on the counter and
sighed.

"I knew my marriage was in trouble
while we stood in the reception line right
after the wedding," she said. "My husband
introduced me to this stringy-haired, buxom
blonde as 'the girl I almost married.' It's been
a real struggle ever since."

Do you remember the first day, the first
moment, you recognized a flaw in your marriage? It might have been a slight difficulty,
barely noticeable at first, like a tiny chip on a
fine china plate.

How long did it take for you to see signs
of unrest? Two years? Two months? Two
weeks? Just a few hours?

It doesn't matter how long it took for

you to notice problems. All marriages, like gardens, require weeding and planting. The need for improvement never ends—if you want one of the good marriages. But right now you may be wondering, *Is it too late? Have I waited too long for repairs?*

Not at all. If you're still married, you can still work on improvements. This study booklet is for your marriage, at whatever stage it's reached. It's for any woman who wants to keep working, to keep trying.

All marriages are in the process of working out a conflict, a disappointment, a failure. So don't hide this booklet under a newspaper or *Time* magazine. Take it to the doctor's waiting room or to aerobics class. You'll be surprised how many women say, "Wow, I sure need to read that!"

It's okay to let others know that you're serious, that you want the very best from your marriage.

So how can you benefit from this study guide?

- Read the whole thing, cover to cover. Cram during your lunch break, during commercials, or while you're sitting under the curling iron. This will provide a helpful, quick overview of the contents.

- Reread the main article, "Where Did Things Go Wrong?" Consider how each point applies to your current situation.

- Work through the "Evaluation" and Bible study lessons, one per week. Consider each biblical passage. Thoughtfully answer each question. Pray. Allow the Lord to reveal how you can strengthen your marriage.

- Jot down key points from the resource sections. Circle books you'd like to read from the bibliography.

- Find a partner, or partners, who will complete this study with you. Use it with your Bible study group, Sunday school class, or your best friend. Ask your partner(s) to help you put the study's principles into practice.

Can a study booklet like this solve all of your marital problems?

Of course not. But with God's grace, it can help. Maybe a lot.

So do yourself a big favor. Take time to gain new insights about yourself and your marriage. And regain your hope in the adventures of matrimony. ■

—JANET CHESTER BLY

Where Did Things Go Wrong?

Even good marriages can hit roadblocks.

Nobody's marriage is perfect.

But everyone seems to want a perfect marriage, anyway.

We wait and hope and work and pray for things to change. But even when they do, something else pops up, and we have to start all over again. With some big crisis or even a little irritation, we catch ourselves whining, "This marriage would be so great, if only. . . ." And we fill in the blank with our current marital problem.

Does this sound like you? You're not alone. Meet Margaret and Ben.

MARGARET AND BEN

"Please pray that Ben will stop drinking."

Margaret gave that same prayer request week after week in our home Bible study group. Because of Ben's alcohol problem, she was trapped in a miserable cycle of anxiety and failure. And we were all eager to support and pray for her.

"You know," Margaret would say, "if only Ben wouldn't drink, our relationship would be so great!"

In one sense, Margaret had an advantage over many wives. She could identify one specific problem in her marriage. She just had to motivate Ben to want to change and to find professional help.

Then two years ago, Margaret announced, "Ben checked himself into a detox center!"

We felt amazed and delighted. Our prayers for Margaret had been answered. We eagerly waited for the miraculous benefits to her family.

Then came the shocker: Margaret still had marital problems.

As long as Ben had been drinking, Margaret had blamed everything on the liquor. But now he was still hard to live with. She didn't know how to cope with the sober Ben, either.

Margaret felt Ben was too authoritative with Benny, Jr. Ben had plunged overboard with a health and fitness kick, while hinting that Margaret was pudgy. And he was underfoot in the evenings—a time when she used to be alone.

To learn to live together, Margaret and Ben had to start from scratch.

"I feel I haven't gained anything," she

sobbed one evening at the Bible study.
"Doesn't it ever smooth out so you can just
relax and enjoy each other? Is this all there
ever is?"

Margaret has discovered that her marriage isn't a one-problem issue. It's beginning
to look like a lifetime challenge.

ANNIE AND KURT

Changes of all kinds can stress the best of
marriages.

Take Annie and Kurt, for example.
They had the model marriage as far as
their friends were concerned. They'd both
graduated from law school, passed the bar,
and joined the same firm. Within a year,
they'd purchased a roomy Tudor house. They
carefully scheduled when they'd have two
children. And they'd established a wise, far-
reaching investment and savings plan.

Meanwhile, they'd developed their prac-
tices, led local charities, hosted luncheons
for dignitaries, even judged the county music
festival. They became a sought-after, attrac-
tive, compatible team.

Then the unexpected happened. Annie
began attending a weekly neighborhood Bible
study while Kurt played in the city basket-
ball league. Within a matter of weeks, Annie
was startled to realize that Jesus offered her
well-ordered life a personal challenge. She
couldn't resist the tremendous tug. She qui-
etly committed her life to Christ.

Annie began to understand spiritual

truth. Immediately, her interests changed. She attended church. She told people, including Kurt, about her amazing discovery.

But Kurt didn't share her enthusiasm. He liked the "old" Annie. He resented her dedication to something he didn't believe in or understand.

"I love my husband," Annie says, "but we're going in two different directions. Is there any hope for us?"

Annie is learning that circumstances alter marriages. New horizons beckon. People change. Couples don't always share similar spiritual commitments. So adjustments must accommodate the shifting forms of a growing marriage.

EMILY AND DAN

For couples like Emily and Dan, a marriage can seem doomed from the start.

Within three weeks after the wedding, Emily realized she'd made a terrible mistake. Dan clashed with her on almost every major discussion.

She wanted a more dependable car to drive to work; he insisted on buying a boat instead. She wanted to attend Sunday school and church every week; he thought once a month was enough. She wanted to finish night classes to become eligible for a management intern program; he insisted her secretarial job was sufficient.

Emily felt overwhelmed. "Why can't

we have it as easy as my folks did?" she wondered. "They always seemed to agree on everything."

Emily has discovered that communication isn't easy. It takes work to create mutual goals and dreams.

IMPERFECT PEOPLE

Imperfect marriages. Some are easy to spot. Others are well-hidden. Some marriage relationships are more imperfect than others. But one thing's for sure: People aren't perfect. And marriage bonds together two imperfect people.

People fall short of what they want to be—or what their spouses expect of them. People disappoint each other and feel disappointed in marriage.

But why? The Bible explains it clearly. Romans 3:12 says, "All have turned away, they have together become worthless; there is no one who does good, not even one." Verse 23 explains, "For all have sinned and fall short of the glory of God."

The Bible says we're sinners. And when we live with someone, there's little we can hide. In marriage, sinful natures surface in one way or another.

Sin is rebellion against God. It's trusting in only yourself. It's a failure to do right and a persistence in doing wrong. It shows up first in our thoughts, then it's revealed by words and actions.

Sin separates. It tears us away from

God. It messes up our relationships, including our marriages.

With sin as a part of every relationship, why do some marriages make it, while others fail? Why do some marriages thrive, while others barely survive? More to the point, how can we be sure our imperfect marriages will last?

We can begin by comprehending God's purposes for marriage.

Some marriages miss the mark because we can't identify the mark in the first place. That is, we don't understand God's purposes for marriage, so we try to make matrimony something it wasn't meant to be. Here's what the Bible says about God's purposes for marriage.

CARING AND COMPANIONSHIP

"The LORD God said, 'It is not good for the man to be alone'" (Genesis 2:18).

People need people. Our purpose and fulfillment in life is not found in isolation, but in interaction with others. So marriage meets the core, basic need of shared company, of knowing that someone in this vast, busy world really cares.

A woman who married at age forty-five recently told me, "Now I know when I go home there will be someone there. It's nice to find a light in the window. A greeting. A 'How was your day?' A friendly human sound other than the television. I knew getting married would bring big changes,

but it's the little things I'm learning to
love the most."

PROCREATION AND COMPLETION

"God blessed them and said to them, 'Be
fruitful and increase in number; fill the earth
and subdue it'" (Genesis 1:28).

We can readily agree that the human
race has fulfilled this command. Today
there's no crying need for more people on
the earth. And many couples have chosen to
remain childless.

But most couples still choose to invest in
the nurture of children. Many fight for the
privilege of furthering the family line into
another generation. A maternal instinct still
surges through most women today.

Mary Ann knows that drive very well.
She's just been talking to her sister, a mother
of five children.

"Mary Ann, don't try so hard," her sister
pleads. "There's so much you have to give.
You don't need a child to prove yourself."

In an hour Mary Ann will suffer her
fifth surgery to try to correct her infertil-
ity. "If only I could have a baby of my own,
then I would be happy," she assures her
husband.

Mary Ann echoes the lament of her biblical sisters, Hannah and Rachel, centuries
before her. She longs for the sense of comple-
tion—the fulfillment that childbearing can
bring to herself and marriage. She wants to
share in God's creative process.

"I will make a helper suitable for him" (Genesis 2:18).

Couples can "share the load" and work together to build a home and provide an income for themselves and their children. They can be aids, attendants, coworkers with each other.

Toni finally relaxed about her imperfect marriage when she learned to appreciate its give-and-take friendship.

"I know my husband would never get to work on time every day without me flying around the house, looking for his keys and glasses. He won't go to any social functions unless I agree to do all the visiting and let him sit in a corner and eat," she explains.

"But I also know I never would have completed that psychology course unless he had fed the dog, bathed the kids, and microwaved his own dinner one night a week."

Simple acts of kindness. Helping hands. These are the right stuff for an amiable relationship. And it's the grace that smooths the rough edges of marriage.

BECOMING ONE FLESH

"For this reason a man will leave his father and mother and be united to his wife, and they will become one flesh" (Genesis 2:24).

The harmony, the cadence, the heartbeat of any marriage must be learned—through practice, through trial and error, through discovering what makes two individuals become a unit. It's getting in sync as a team.

Some marriages appear to outsiders as effortless as pairs of Olympic ice skaters. But we don't see the tears, the trials, the endless rehearsals. We just see the public performance, not the private pains that have been pricked and healed over the years.

Oneness in marriage requires a measure of separation from all others, beginning with our parents.

"I don't think Jim really had ever left his mom emotionally," Barbara confided. "The best thing that happened to our marriage was moving clear across the country when he was offered a promotion. He's finally attempting to make decisions without seeking her approval on every little thing. And the long-distance phone calls are only twice a month now."

Marriage demands adult participants. Maturity means giving up the parental nest and striking out on our own. Becoming one conveys letting go of one arm and clutching tight to another.

Oneness also implies sexual faithfulness. Stephanie recalls, "During a time when Tim and I were having some troubles, one of his friends offered to paint our house for us on his free hours. And so this friend spent most of a month hanging around. He was so understanding, so willing to listen—everything I wished Tim would be, but wasn't. Then one day he gave me one of *those looks*.

"I knew what might be coming next. All I

had to do was give him some encouragement. And I was sure tempted. He looked so good to me right then. But one thing held me back. I knew it would just about kill Tim if he ever found out. I couldn't do that to him." So Stephanie politely but firmly turned her back on Tim's friend.

"Thanks to God, our marriage is so much better now, and I don't have a guilty conscience hanging over me," she says.

TRUE LOVE

"Husbands, love your wives, just as Christ loved the church and gave himself up for her" (Ephesians 5:25).

Marriage provides a private, intimate look into sacrificial love, a glimpse into the mysteries of Christ's desire for us. A faithful, lifetime partner witnesses our despicable faults and sins, yet still values us by toughing it out over the years. Such human love is a taste of God's divine passion. Marriage provides a living object lesson of spiritual truth.

"Marriage is a schoolroom, not a playground," said Henry Drummond, a nineteenth-century Scottish evangelist.[1] While we hope for plenty of recesses and fun, marriage often exposes our selfish natures and forces us to change. It's the most immediate opportunity for practicing the spiritual knowledge stuffed inside us. Marriage provides the ultimate test for proving God's principles for living.

In his book *Harmony in Marriage,* Leland Wood sums up this marriage-as-education approach: "As there are many things to learn about marriage and few persons have been educated for this art in any adequate way, the husband and wife must take the attitude of learners, finding out gradually how to live together at their best." [2]

FACING DISAPPOINTMENTS

So why does marriage disappoint us? Perhaps it's because the man snoring in bed every night only slightly resembles the before-marriage suitor.

Instead of a virile, freshly showered charmer at the door, there's a pile of dirty underwear in the corner. Instead of mousse and Châteaubriand by candlelight, there's a half-full milk carton spoiling on the kitchen counter. Instead of an evening filled with the scents of Ralph Lauren and Charlie, there're morning burps and bad breath.

It hits hardest on the first "date" after marriage. Before, we primped and prepared, leisurely and alone. Now, he yells for his tie, wonders why there are no clean socks in his drawer, tells you to hurry up, and begs for extra cash from the grocery allowance. It resembles a domestic duel more than a lovers' getaway.

Without our realizing it, our high expectations tumble into the lowly realities of living together, day by day.

Romance movies and books don't help a bit. They always end *at the wedding*. There's a lot of living and giving needed to make a marriage after the celebration.

Often we expect love to accomplish more than it can. We think it should cause a relationship to soar higher, deepen faster, and soften quicker than any other social interchange. And love *does* do that. But not by itself. With skill and care, the relationship has to be nurtured in a million different, daily, mundane ways.

But finding a less-than-perfect reality doesn't have to mean losing a marriage. It's a prime transition point that can transform each of us. When we tell ourselves and God the truth about the situation, He can help us work together for essential improvement. The marriage may never be perfect, but the situation can get better.

WORKING TOWARD CHANGE

Working toward change is a step-by-step process. There are no instant cures for disappointing marriages. But little by little, we can turn small irritations into big opportunities for growth and change.

❑ **Tackle one problem.** There may be a number of distresses in a marriage, but the chances of overhauling them all at once are slim. Confront only one conflict at a time.

❑ **Talk about the problem.** In as calm and considerate a way as possible, talk together about what's wrong. If your spouse is a believer, talk about why this situation hinders God's goals for marriage. Don't mention a pile of grievances; talk about just this one. Offer ideas for how to solve this marriage dilemma.

❏ **Take a look inside.** While talking together about the problem, ask for advice. How could both partners help in the matter? Better yet, how do you contribute to the problem? Is there something about you that your husband would really like to change? Receive the criticism and get busy on a program of self-discipline.

Margaret's husband Ben finally conquered alcoholism. Now that he's sober, Margaret realizes she had blamed her own failures on Ben's drinking. In the light of his big change, she's forced to deal with her deficiencies. One by one, she's making progress.

A perfect marriage? No. But Margaret and Ben are different people than they were two years ago. They're gradually stretching and expanding their love for each other.

❏ **Assess the magnitude.** Is this a deep-seated, traumatic, long-term problem? Or could it be an everyday, temporary situation? Discerning the difference helps create an effective response.

Write out a description of what's wrong in the marriage and what has to change. Then ask, "Is this a major cause, or a minor symptom? Will this current difficulty last indefinitely, or is there a built-in time limit?"

If the problem will fade with time, can it be tolerated until it's over? When was there a similar trial of this length before? Can the same survival tactics apply here? Recall and list the insights and benefits from your former experience.

In the meantime, if the difficulty is long-term, what could make it more tolerable? The common cold isn't curable yet, but available medicine makes the symptoms bearable. Perhaps the same could be true in marriage. Look for small actions, words, or ways of thinking that could lessen the overall stress. Don't expect quick, dramatic results, but prepare to rejoice over every small triumph.

MAKING ASSESSMENTS

Margaret's making these assessments. She's discovering her mixed-up priorities— and the difference between dealing with *faults, diversities,* and *sins.*

Faults are habits, blemishes, or chronic disabilities that detract from a person's overall appeal. But they can and should be tolerated, if possible, in loving relationships. Ben's obsession with fitness could be a fault, but Margaret's waiting to see if it's a temporary fetish, a backlash to his years of bombing his body with alcohol.

Diversities are personality distinctions that characterize a certain viewpoint and response to life's challenges and decisions. These differences can bring healthy expansions of each individual's way of seeing and doing things. Diversities should be welcomed in marriage.

24

Margaret and Ben's clash on how to discipline Benny, Jr., pivots on diversity—a difference in their backgrounds, personalities, and goals for Ben. Only the drunkenness was a sin.

Often diversities that attract people to each other hide corresponding faults. For instance, sensitivity and understanding for people with hardships may make a mate overly generous with time and possessions.

But *sins* need to be confronted. These are actions forbidden by Scripture, defects in character that could lead to evil consequences.

Ben's trip to the detox center made him confront sin. Now whenever it gets really tough, Margaret drives by the courthouse and jail. It's been over two years since she bailed Ben out. She knows things are better than they used to be, no matter how unpleasant certain moments might seem.

❏ **Tap into spiritual resources.** Making a good marriage requires a working, practicing confidence in God's supernatural power. So study the Scriptures. Trust God. Believe Him. Acknowledge His presence and participation in daily life. Fight Satan, the enemy of marriage, with the whole armor of God (Ephesians 6:13-18). Explore God's answers to the deep-rooted, sinful problems in your marriage.

Faithfully pray, asking God for insight to understand each other's needs; for strength and creativity day by day to do what's required; and for ways to love each other while dealing with problems.

Annie's husband, Kurt, resented her conversion to Christ, so she saved her exuberance for friends and kept quiet and gentle about her faith at home. That's been hard for her. Sometimes she wants to scream the truth at Kurt. But she's found an understanding prayer partner, whom she can call anytime. And inch by inch, the marriage grows again.

Another couple struggling with difficulties in their marriage made the commitment to pray aloud in bed each night in each other's arms. This activity enabled them to turn a corner in their marriage; they began to open up and share their thoughts and feelings.

In his book *Sex Begins in the Kitchen,* Dr. Kevin Leman explains the results: "A special warmth and closeness of being in each other's arms and holding each other followed. Their stresses, problems, fears and worries were taken to God in prayer, together. Not only did their communication with each other improve, but their communication and openness with God became a mighty, working force in both their lives."[3]

The support of a mentor, fellow sufferer, or a group could also relieve tensions. So ask a pastor, Christian counselor, or mature Christian friend to be a mentor or to recommend a fellowship.

❏ **Give the problem time.** Keep alert to God's insights—the big picture of what

He may be trying to accomplish in your marriage. Meanwhile, don't keep bringing up the subject again and again, pounding the issue into the ground. Instead, recognize improvements and give praise where it's due.

One day Emily got so angry with her husband's stubbornness that she locked herself in the bathroom.

"I'm not coming out until I've decided to leave Dan, kill myself, or completely accept this situation as God's will for me," she cried.

Four hours and a box of tissues later, she emerged.

"I finally decided, no matter how frustrated I got, I wasn't going to commit suicide or walk out," she said. "With those two options eliminated, that meant I had to find a way to accept these impasses, and work them through. Maybe that's what the Lord had in mind all along when He brought Dan into my life. He wanted me to stop running away from crises and to grow up."

Now Emily sees each day as part of God's plan, complete with Dan's complications. It took her months to get used to that idea, and years to express mature responses. But Emily's surviving. In fact, she'll admit, "We're growing closer than I ever imagined we could."

❏ **Find ways to keep growing.** Study. Play. Exercise. Take a class. Spend time helping at the convalescent hospital. Take your child on a field trip. Do anything but mope and stew at home or work, ready to pounce on your spouse.

Nobody's perfect. But imperfect marriages can grow, even thrive. They can prove the power of Christ.

If we let Him, the perfect Christ can fill the gaps of our imperfections. He can complete His purposes in our lives through our commitment to another fragile human. That's when His glory shines. That's when we're right where He wanted us: imperfect, but growing. ■

NOTES
1. Henry Drummond, *The Greatest Thing in the World* (New York: The Peter Pauper Press, n.d.), page 37.
2. Leland Foster Wood, *Harmony in Marriage* (New York: Round Table Press, 1960), page 2.
3. Kevin Leman, *Sex Begins in the Kitchen* (Ventura, CA: Regal Books, 1981), page 88.

How Imperfect Is Your Marriage?

Find out if you're for better or for worse.

Why did you marry?

Because you were in love? Because you couldn't live without sex? Because it was expected? Because you wanted a man's influence? Because you longed to be needed?

Is your original reason still the basis for a relationship with your husband? Or have your requirements changed over the years?

Sometimes disappointment in marriage follows changes in desires, values, or circumstances. Explore what's happening in your marriage.

ASSESSING SYMPTOMS

1. The following statements are common symptoms of a marriage that needs to

grow. Mark the statements that sound
the most like you.

❏ "The Petersons have a great marriage,
and our relationship is nothing like
theirs." (Comparison)

❏ "We used to be much closer when
we first got married. Now we both
seem to be going our separate ways."
(Stagnation)

❏ "We can never agree on the important
things in life—like disciplining the
children, how to spend the money, sex,
religious commitment." (Disunity)

❏ "I shouldn't have to put up with his
constant verbal abuse." (Disrespect)

❏ "I have needs that aren't being met. I
feel unfulfilled." (Frustration)

❏ Add your own:

2. Think about the statements you checked
   and the problems in parentheses that
   they represent. How else does your marriage express comparison, stagnation,
   disunity, disrespect, or frustration?

BUILT-IN TIME BOMBS

3. Relational problems don't develop
   overnight. Often what you bring to a
   marriage affects its growth. Some marital time bombs are listed below. Check
   the problems that were brought into your
   marriage.

   ❑ Chronic illness

   ❑ Substance abuse

   ❑ Alienation from God

   ❑ Previous marriage(s)

   ❑ Bitterness over past hurts

❏ No or little outside interests

❏ Sex/children outside of marriage

❏ Self-image (either too high or too low)

❏ Unresolved complications with parents

❏ Other:

4. Could any of the time bombs you checked have contributed to the problems in question 1? If so, in what ways?

COMMEND THE GOOD

5. Does your marriage achieve God's purposes? Rate the areas in the following test—alone or, if you're brave enough, with your husband. Circle the appropriate number when "1" equals poor and "10" equals perfect.

Companionship. Does your husband provide you with companionship?

1   2   3   4   5   6   7   8   9   10

Ask him to rate you in the same area.

1   2   3   4   5   6   7   8   9   10

Procreation. Has your desire to have children—or not to have children—been met?

1   2   3   4   5   6   7   8   9   10

How does your husband respond to this same question?

1   2   3   4   5   6   7   8   9   10

Mutual assistance. Does your husband meet your need for assistance in the struggles of being wife, mother, woman?

1   2   3   4   5   6   7   8   9   10

How does he rate your assistance to him?

1   2   3   4   5   6   7   8   9   10

Oneness. Rate yourself on a unity scale. Are you living in harmony?

1   2   3   4   5   6   7   8   9   10

What is his opinion?

1   2   3   4   5   6   7   8   9   10

Practicing true love. Does your demonstration of love toward each other resemble Christ's love for the church?

1   2   3   4   5   6   7   8   9   10

How does your husband see it?

1   2   3   4   5   6   7   8   9   10

RATE YOUR RESULTS

Now add up your points and double them to see how close you come to the ideal. Score: _____.

In comparison, double your husband's points to see how he rates your relationship. Notice the similarities and differences in your opinions. Score: _____.

Also add your original points (before you doubled them) to your husband's original points. The total will probably be a closer view of how you both feel about your marriage. Score: _____.

Here's how to interpret your scores:

SCORE	INTERPRETATION
90-100	You're as close to heaven as you're going to get.
70-90	Your marriage is the envy of the neighborhood.
50-70	You have good potential for quick growth.
30-50	There's a lot of room for steady improvement.
10-30	Growing your marriage should be your highest concern.
0-10	No debate, your marriage exists in name only. But with God's help, it's not hopeless!

No matter your scores, accept where your marriage is now. Pledge yourself to take positive steps that will lift that total, point by point, year by year.

BEGIN A JOURNEY

6. Begin your journey toward better matrimony by listing the changes you would like to see in your marriage.

7. Write a few sentences about what it will take to make these adjustments.

8. Write a prayer to God, asking Him to help you work toward a better marriage. ■

Toughing It Out

Accepting an imperfect husband.

As with all problems, there are surface symptoms and root causes in a marriage. Sometimes we blame marriage as the tension producer of our lives, when we're really coping with personal, inner struggles.

Or sometimes we fall apart adjusting to a less-than-perfect man, when we should realize that all people are imperfect—and that our marriage might actually be normal.

The root cause of your marital dissatisfaction can lie within yourself, your mate, or both of you. But you can't come to terms with the whole situation until you can clearly state what's wrong.

HUSBAND HASSLES

1. List your current aggravations and challenges, dividing them between

37

personal hassles and hassles with your
husband.

PERSONAL HASSLES	HUSBAND HASSLES

2. Which of the above problems affect your
   marriage relationship? Mark each with
   an "M." Which of these are of primary
   importance to solve? Circle them.

3. How could you determine if your problems are serious or just the common ups
   and downs of most marriages?

4. a. Make a list of five characteristics or
actions that bother you about yourself
and about your husband.

MY NEGATIVE TRAITS	HIS NEGATIVE TRAITS

b. How are these negative traits affecting
your marriage?

5. Taking your cues from the definitions on
pages 24-25, categorize each of the above

traits as either faults, personality differences, or sins.

FAULTS	DIFFERENCES	SINS
Mine		
His		

6. How would you like your husband to respond to your faults, differences, and sins? Are you responding the same way to him? Explain.

7. According to the verses below, how does God want you to respond to your mate's faults and differences?

Romans 12:3-6a

Ephesians 4:32

Philippians 2:1-4

James 5:9-11

8. How would God have you respond to your mate's sins?

Luke 6:37,41-42

Galatians 6:1-5

James 5:16

9. How could you learn to respond in a loving manner to your husband's weaknesses listed in questions 4 and 5?

POSITIVE TRAITS

10. Make a list of positive traits in both you and your husband.

MY POSITIVE TRAITS	HIS POSITIVE TRAITS

11. How can these positive traits help overcome the negative aspects of your marriage? How can you accentuate your own and your husband's positive traits?

ONGOING COMMITMENT

12. a. God takes your marriage seriously. What do these verses reveal about His viewpoint on commitment in marriage?

    Matthew 19:3-9

    Romans 7:2

    1 Corinthians 7:12-14

Hebrews 13:4

b. How do you feel about this instruction? What specific direction do any of these verses give you for your own marriage?

13. How willing are you to tough it out and work through your marriage disappointments? Is this willingness based on certain conditions? Explain.

LOOKING AHEAD

14. Consider and list the benefits that resulted from other hard times in your life. What lessons did you learn?

DIFFICULT TIME	LESSON

15. What good things could result through your current marriage disappointments?

16. What promise from the Bible can you claim as you prepare to work through your marriage difficulties?

- This week, interview an older woman about past disappointments in her marriage. How did she get through them? What were the rewards of persevering? How does she feel about those struggles today? Consider how her insights can help you.

- The next time you get really outraged about your marriage, march into the bathroom with a notebook. Stare into the mirror, and write down a complete description of your facial expression. Later, when you've cooled off, read your description out loud. How does it make you feel?

- On a separate piece of paper, copy the list of priority hassles and negative traits that affect your marriage. Which problems require (a) changes in your spouse; (b) changes in your attitude toward him; (c) both? Based on God's Word, decide how you can begin approaching these priority problems. ∎

Forgiveness That Makes a Difference

*Giving him another chance
to change.*

There's an art . . . a grace to learning to live
together. The Bible says a lot about being
patient, tenderhearted, and compassionate
toward each other.

We're commanded to practice the craft of
forgiving. In other words, we're to give room
in our relationships for mutual humanity.
And that's especially true in marriage.

As you begin to study this lesson on
forgiveness, your thoughts may already be
crowded with problem areas in your marriage where your husband's humanity seems
obvious, and you desire to have an attitude of
forgiveness.

GREAT EXPECTATIONS

1. a. What were your expectations for
marriage? Make a detailed list and

47

put a mark by the ones that are being
fulfilled presently.

b. What could these expectations reveal
about you?

2. How do you feel about the unmet expectations in your marriage?

3. Could your unmet expectations affect your willingnesss to forgive? If so, how?

4. a. In the chart below, answer the following questions.

   • What are the three toughest situations you've ever had to forgive?

   • How did your expectations affect each of these situations?

SITUATION	EXPECTATIONS

b. What can you learn from these past
   situations to help you forgive now?

PREVENTIVE ATTITUDES

5. Unrealistic expectations and selfishness
   can prevent you from forgiving someone.
   What other barriers may be preventing
   you from forgiving your husband?

6. Read Luke 23:33-35.

   a. When did Christ forgive His
      persecutors?

   b. What attitudes must have enabled
      Him to forgive?

c. How can you apply Christ's example to your marriage?

7. Study each of the following scriptures and determine why it's crucial to forgive people who hurt you.

Mark 11:25-26

2 Corinthians 2:5-8

Hebrews 12:14-15

DAILY DOSES

How do you begin to give each other a break for the day-to-day irritations? How do you keep them from ballooning into insurmountable problems?

It involves daily doses of forgiveness— and remembering the principles in bold type on the following pages.

To forgive him, you don't need to wait until your husband confesses.

8. Read Luke 23:34 again.

a. Did Jesus' forgiveness excuse the people's actions? Explain.

b. Why did Christ forgive when His offenders didn't confess?

Sometimes you will need to forgive your husband repeatedly.

9. Read Matthew 18:21-22.

a. Did Jesus intend that you keep a record of how many times you forgive? Explain.

b. In light of recurring problems with your husband, how does Christ's instruction make you feel?

If you're really going to forgive, you'll begin with a decision of the heart.

10. a. Read the following verses. What do they say about the heart (inner person)?

   Matthew 15:18

   1 Peter 1:22

   b. Based on these verses, how does the condition of your heart relate to your ability to forgive?

   c. Is it your responsibility to change the condition of the offender's heart? Explain.

Forgiving can be tough, but it's not impossible!

11. According to these verses, why is it possible for you to forgive?

    Matthew 19:26

    Romans 8:37-39

    Colossians 3:13-15

INCREASED FAITH

12. Read Luke 17:4-5.

    a. What did Jesus say that brought about the apostles' plea for more faith?

b. Why might forgiveness require an increase in faith?

c. According to verse 6, how much faith does it take to forgive?

13. Why can it be difficult to express even a small amount of faith, so you can forgive?

14. a. According to Romans 10:17, how can you increase your faith? List practical ways you can follow the instruction in this verse.

b. What other ways can you strengthen your faith so you will forgive?

LOOKING AT YOU

15. Read 1 Peter 3:3-4, and consider the qualities that are of great worth to God.

   a. Do most people today value these qualities? Do you? Explain.

   b. If you allowed these qualities to dominate your life, could it affect your ability to forgive? Explain.

16. Forgiving others also means forgiving yourself. Think of the most difficult situation you currently face in forgiving your husband.

   a. Could your actions have contributed to this problem? If so, how?

   b. Have you asked God to forgive your personal failures in this situation? Have you forgiven yourself? If not, write a prayer requesting forgiveness.

17. Forgiving others allows the perfect justice of God to take place. It allows Him to work His will in a situation. How do these verses relate to forgiveness?

Leviticus 19:18

Psalm 103:8-10,12

Romans 12:19

2 Peter 3:9

Forgiving includes giving yourself time to get over the shock of the wrong done and to work through your emotions and feelings.

Forgiveness also allows the matter to be committed to God, rather than taking things into your own hands.

FORGIVING THIS WEEK

• How many "free mistakes" do you allow your husband in a day? A free mistake is when he obviously errs, but you refuse to bring it up to him, tell others what he has done, or sit around thinking about it.

How many free mistakes would you like to receive from him each day?

This week, allow him just as many free mistakes as you'd appreciate. If you're really feeling generous, grant him double that amount.

• Ask this question of the people with whom you spend the most time during a normal week: "In comparison to others, do you think I am a little too slow to forgive; about average in forgiving; or quick to forgive?" What conclusion can you draw from their answers?

• Pick out your toughest marital situation to forgive. What will your life be like if this is never resolved? How do you feel about this? Write out your answers.

• Consider the statement on the following page. How does your marriage compare to it? If you're unhappy with your answer, what changes do you need to make?

*A husband does not need a yes woman;
he needs a companion willing to respect
him enough to be her own person and
tell him who she really is and what she
really thinks. A wife should be able to be
in her husband's presence essentially who
she is in his absence.*[1] ∎

NOTE
  1. Nancy Groom, *Married Without Masks* (Colorado
     Springs, CO: NavPress, 1989), page 37.

Old-Fashioned Problem Solving

*Praying about your
marriage problems.*

Problem solving in marriage involves confrontation, discussion, knowing when to stay silent, and when to take action. But first, you must begin with prayer.

"Go home and pray about it" is not a wimpy response to marital problems. It's the greatest spiritual advice you can follow. The old adage is true: Prayer changes things.

FIRST THINGS FIRST

1. According to these verses, why is it crucial to pray about marital problems?

   Psalm 119:143-148

Romans 8:24-27

Colossians 1:9-12

2. How's your prayer life for your husband?
   Check the descriptions that apply to you.

   Prayer for my husband is . . .

   ❏ not something he deserves.

   ❏ a vital part of my everyday life.

   ❏ something I activate during
      emergencies.

   ❏ a normal segment of my spiritual
      routine.

   ❏ something I seldom think of for my
      husband.

   ❏ something I've grown weary of because
      I never see any changes.

   ❏ other:

3. a. What barriers exist in praying for your husband?

   b. How could prayer affect those barriers?

4. What if the Lord only knew of your husband by what you told Him in prayer? On the next page, list things about your husband that you're always telling the Lord. Then list five things you don't mention to God about your husband, but should.

WHAT I SAY	WHAT I DON'T SAY

5. What do these lists reveal about your attitude toward your husband? Could your prayers affect your attitude? Explain.

HOW TO PRAY

To keep your talks with God from turning into constant gripe sessions, you may want to balance your prayers for your husband. For every problem or negative trait of his you bring up, offer thanks for a positive trait as well. Use the positive traits you listed on page 42 as a guide.

6. As you read through the verses below, determine how you should pursue praying for your husband.

Matthew 6:6-8

Matthew 7:7-8

Matthew 18:19-20

John 14:13-14

7. What attitudes are important as you pray?

Mark 11:24-25

1 Thessalonians 5:16-18

James 4:3

8. What will happen when you pray?

Hebrews 7:25

1 John 5:14-15

9. Read Jesus' parable in Luke 18:1-8.

   a. What does it show about perseverance in prayer?

   b. What's your response?

10. How could you use the Lord's Prayer in Matthew 6:9-13 as a guide in prayer for your husband?

11. To be a better wife, what changes do you need to make?

12. How could these changes alter your disappointment in marriage?

13. Make a list of what needs to change in you and your husband so your marriage can improve.

IN ME	IN HIM

14. What sins do you personally need to confess in order to change?

A LOOK AT YOU

Sometimes praying for our husbands' faults can help us avoid what needs to change in ourselves. And often God wants to change us as much as we want to change our husbands.

15. What are your motives in praying for changes in your marriage and in your husband?

16. Are you willing to trust God and to continue in your marriage, even if your prayers aren't answered? Explain.

17. Prayer for your marriage shouldn't just focus on getting you or your husband to change. Prayer involves praise, confession, intercession, and personal requests. Using the following chart as a guide, develop a prayer list for your marriage. Keep the list and note progress or the date each request is answered.

Marriage Prayer List

Praise to God for my marriage:

Confession of my sins:

Intercession for my husband:

Requests for myself:

GETTING HELP

How do you find a good prayer partner to help you pray for your marriage? The first step is obvious. Pray for one.

- This week, design a profile of a perfect prayer partner for you.

- Which women you know best fit this description?

- Begin praying that the Lord would give you the opportunity to ask one of these women to be your regular prayer partner.

- How does the following quote apply to your marriage?

  We shall draw nearer to God, not by trying to avoid the sufferings inherent in all loves, but by accepting them and offering them to Him; throwing away all defensive armor.[1] ∎

NOTE

1. C. S. Lewis, *The Four Loves* (New York: Harcourt Brace Jovanovich, 1960), page 170.

Life Beyond Today

*Creating a union that lasts
a lifetime.*

According to recent surveys, the highest percentage of happily wedded women were thirty to thirty-four years old when they married.

But what makes people truly happy in matrimony is not age, but attitude. For example, an inflamed ego will threaten a marriage very quickly. The pride and stubbornness of ego can control partners so they care little about what happens—now or in the future.

HEZEKIAH SYNDROME

Once the honeymoon is over—and especially when a partnership gets rocky—it's tempting to forget God as the foundation of a marriage.

A woman, who once prayed desperately for a husband, now might whine, "I deserve better than this!" Or if things go well, she might forget that God is the source of all good gifts (James 1:17). In both cases, ego protrudes and she takes the marriage into her own hands.

King Hezekiah had the same problem in regard to his kingdom.

1. Study Isaiah 38 and 39.

   a. What was Hezekiah's problem? (38:1)

   b. How did he ask God to help him? (38:2-3)

   c. How did God answer him? (38:4-5)

   d. What was Hezekiah's initial response? (38:9-14)

e. How did Hezekiah forget God and let ego take over? (39:1-2)

f. What were the results of Hezekiah's egotistical actions? (39:5-7)

g. What was shortsighted about Hezekiah's response? (39:8)

SHORT-TERM MISTAKES

Hezekiah might have been relieved over the short-term resolution to his problem. But his attitude left nothing behind for the next generation to build upon.

The same mistake can be made in a marriage. Our need for immediate relief or gratification can eclipse future rewards and security—for ourselves, for our children, for the solidity of marriage for couples in the future. Instead, we need to develop a long-range view of what a marriage can reap in years to come.

2. Besides ego, what other attitudes could cause a wife to become shortsighted in her marriage and give up too quickly? List them below. Then circle the attitudes that might describe you.

3. Name three ways you could react and miss God's purpose during a rough siege in your marriage.

4. Shortsightedness about marriage results from focusing on worldly instead of eternal values.

    Read Philippians 3:7-11. Why did Paul harbor no regrets about losing things that the world considers important?

5. a. Which short-term values do you clutch most frantically in your marriage?

    ❏ Public image

    ❏ Beautiful home

    ❏ Family traditions

    ❏ Personal appearance

    ❏ Financial stability

    ❏ Material possessions

    ❏ Personal satisfaction

    ❏ Being "right" in a conflict

    ❏ Other:

b. Why do you cling to these values?

6. Do any of the above values contribute to your current marriage disappointment?

7. If you were to stop focusing on the short-term values in question 5, what would you need to do? How does this make you feel?

8. Read Ephesians 5:22-33. What does God desire for the marriage relationship? How do you feel about these instructions?

9. How can you focus on God's desires for your marriage?

Psalm 119:7

Psalm 119:60

Psalm 119:173

Proverbs 3:5-7

James 1:21

10. What could be the benefits of focusing on long-range, eternal goals for your marriage?

REAL RESPONSES

11. Suppose a friend has decided to leave her husband. From what you've learned about long-term marriage values, think of a response to each of the following statements. You may want to write your thoughts on a separate piece of paper.

   a. "The world's a mess. What difference will one more divorce make?"

   b. "Hey, my kids are sharp. They'll turn out all right."

   c. "I'm tired of showing him love and getting nothing back in return."

   d. "I made a dumb mistake when I married him. Am I supposed to live with that all my life?"

   e. "I don't care what the Bible says! I'm sure God doesn't want me to go on like this."

f. "I feel so wonderful now that I've made up my mind to divorce him."

g. "I met a man who makes me feel like a princess. I want to be with him. That's what a relationship should be."

12. Develop at least five goals for your marriage that focus on eternal values.

13. List five lifelong lessons you've already learned from your marriage. How can these lessons help you pursue the goals in question 12?

This week, turn to pages 83-85 and read about the marital difficulties of two godly women in "Nobody Said It'd Be Easy!"

Then think about your marriage. At the end of your life, how would you want someone to summarize your response to marriage disappointments? What would you like your marriage to leave behind for future generations? Write your story on a separate sheet of paper.

Read the following quote with this question in mind: Do you have an "alive" marriage?

> *In an alive marriage relationship a wife receives her husband's love with joy, and in response she delights and challenges him with her unique gifts and personality. If, instead, she fears him and sacrifices her personhood by becoming absorbed in his, she will have nothing to give him. Thinking herself biblically submissive, she will actually be cheating him of her love and denying him one of life's greatest pleasures—the blending of two individuals, male and female, into one creative whole. Both lose out when one gets lost.*[1] ■

NOTE
1. Nancy Groom, *Married Without Masks* (Colorado Springs, CO: NavPress, 1989), page 35.

Nobody Said It'd Be Easy!

*Learn from the rocky marriages of
two godly women.*

The marriage relationship has never been
an easy road. Women all through the ages
have had their struggles. Their courage and
stamina can be an inspiration to the women
of our age who need to recapture the glory of
meeting their own appointed challenge.

JEANNE GUYON (1648-1717)

Married at sixteen, Jeanne Guyon entered
a house of discord. If she expressed an
opinion, her mother-in-law accused her of
starting a dispute, compelled her to perform
humiliating tasks, and gave the servants
precedence over her.

The mother-in-law carried tales to her
son about his young wife. He was sick most
of the time and was cared for by a nurse who
dominated him. The mother-in-law also had

nothing but bitter words about his wife's family.

Jeanne faced this heavy trial by comparing her situation to Joseph's in the Bible. She felt God had placed her in this difficulty for her own good. She believed this tribulation was necessary to accomplish God's purpose in her life.

After twelve years of marriage, Jeanne's husband died, but not before they reconciled the tensions in their relationship. Then Madame Guyon traveled around the world, teaching weary believers effective methods of prayer that she'd learned while imprisoned by hostilities in her own house.[1]

SUSANNA WESLEY (1669-1742)

It has been said of this woman that she had "an almost perfect Christian household." A frail woman, she taught her nineteen children six hours a day for twenty years. Meanwhile, she had to manage the family's extremely tight finances as debts mounted and the family's credit was exhausted.

Never a practical man, her husband could not make ends meet and was imprisoned for his inability to pay the bills. His wife took full charge of feeding the family and caring for their dairy herd, pigs, and hens—their only means of support at that time.

Susanna instilled in all of her children a passion for learning. She understood better than her husband the needs and dreams of their children, for she had both sensitive perception and womanly intuition. She was the stronger personality, but she chose to be a loyal wife who never lost sight of her husband's good points and never carped at him for his bad management of family affairs and mounting debts.

Her philosophy of life was this: "Though man is born to trouble, yet I believe there is scarce a man to be found upon earth but, take the whole course of his life, hath more mercies than afflictions, and much more pleasure than pain."[2]

FINDING PEACE

Becoming a team in the midst of disappointments, finding the peace despite the differences that won't change, that's the unique calling for any marriage. And for marriages that aren't quite made in heaven that same challenge can entice, invigorate, and stimulate some of the highest, purest examples of human devotion. ∎

NOTES
  1. Adapted from Edith Deen, *Great Women of the Christian Faith*, "Mme. Jeanne Guyon" (New York: Harper & Brothers Publishers, 1959), pages 130-136.
  2. Adapted from Deen, "Susanna Wesley," pages 141-147.

A New Attitude

*Develop a marriage
praise calendar.*

Every marriage has times of static. You
don't need to chart those scenarios; you'll
remember them. But how easily we forget
the special moments as they're buried under
a mountain of mundane activities.

Here's a way to capture and collect the
shining hours of this next year. Obtain an
inexpensive, yearly calendar that shows the
months at a glance. Don't use it to record the
ordinary events, meetings, appointments,
and other things to do. Instead, use it to jot
down the things in your marriage for which
you can thank and praise God.

Each night (using the same willpower
that ensures your teeth get brushed) grab
your praise calendar and record a note for
that day. Keep it short and positive.

Read the calendar during good and bad
times. It will be a great attitude adjuster
while waiting at the airport, or the dentist's
office, or before church services begin. It
might even change your opinion of your
marriage. ■

Garbage Advice

*How to determine who's giving you
a bum steer.*

Everybody's got advice for you. Radio talk
show hosts, newspaper columnists, your
sister in Houston, and of course, the girls at
the beauty parlor. This study booklet is also
crammed with advice.

So who should you believe? Which advice
should you throw out with the daily garbage?
Try these guidelines:

1. All advice should make sense to you. God
   does not intend to bypass your mind.

2. All advice should make sense to the
   mature Christians who sincerely care
   about you. God does not bypass the community of believers.

3. All advice should sit well, subjectively,
   with your own spirit. ("Deep down inside,

I know it's what I ought to do.") God does
not bypass the Holy Spirit within you.

4. All advice must agree with the text and
   the intent of biblical truth. God does not
   go back on His Word.

5. The best advice is given by people of
   integrity, those who have built a reputa-
   tion of honesty. The truth is mirrored in
   their own lives. If they can't live it, why
   believe it?

6. Godly advice follows a route that leads to
   God receiving glory. This should be the
   ultimate goal of all true believers. ∎

Tackling Special Problems

What to do about sin and abuse.

WHEN YOUR MATE SINS

Before the confrontation:
1. Demonstrate your loyalty. Prove that you are really on his side.

2. Demonstrate your spiritual growth. Put Scripture into open, public practice.

3. Demonstrate your vulnerability. Let him see you are working to overcome your own faults.

During the confrontation:
1. Tell him why you think the action is wrong (Luke 17:3).

2. Rebuke him with patience and instruction (2 Timothy 4:2).

3. Assure him that he doesn't have to face this problem alone (Galatians 6:1-2).

4. Admonish him as a brother, not as an enemy (2 Thessalonians 3:15).

5. Use the wisdom that comes from God (James 3:17).

6. Be careful in your choice of words (Ephesians 4:29, Colossians 4:6).

After the confrontation:
1. Allow your mate to suffer necessary consequences (Galatians 6:7).

2. Give your mate time to repent (Mark 14:66-72, John 21:15-17).

3. Rejoice together when you've worked through the confrontation (1 Peter 1:6).[1]

WHEN CONFLICT BECOMES ABUSE

1. Pray.

2. If your life is threatened, leave the home.

3. Let others know about the problem. Create a network of knowledgeable people who will not be surprised when an incident erupts.

4. Communicate your anger to your husband in the presence of a third party

who can help the listening and hearing process.

5. Determine ahead of time what it will take to cause you to leave your husband.

6. If physical abuse occurs a third time, leave the home. Three times constitutes a pattern.

7. Find a safe place to live.

8. Go to a doctor for medical treatment and verification.

9. Seek a supportive community.

10. Find a Christian counselor.[2] ∎

NOTES
1. Stephen and Janet Bly, *Be Your Mate's Best Friend* (Chicago, IL: Moody Press, 1989), pages 149-159.
2. Kenneth W. Petersen, "Wife Abuse: The Silent Crime, The Silent Church," *Christianity Today*, November 25, 1983, page 24.

Caught in the Middle

How to help your kids feel wanted.

Children in the midst of family conflict have a special need to feel wanted, secure, loved. Consider the following suggestions.

1. Give them eye-to-eye contact.
2. Tell them, "I love you!"
3. Respect their property.
4. Treat each child with equal affection.
5. Give them honest praise.
6. Instill hope. Let them know God is helping your family to work out the problems.
7. Treat their friends as welcome visitors.
8. Be alert to unusual behavior as their way of coping. Let them talk out their feelings. Be willing to seek professional counsel.
9. Forgive their quirks that add stress. Start each day without yesterday's baggage.
10. Deal out fair and consistent discipline.
11. Never put down their father.
12. Allow them to help you in some way. Kids feel wanted when they feel needed.
13. Pray about their private wars—depression, peer pressure, fear of losing you. ■

BIBLIOGRAPHY

Resources for Married People

Books, tapes, and seminars to help both of you.

Backus, William, and Marie Chapian. *Telling Yourself the Truth*. Minneapolis, MN: Bethany Fellowship, 1980.

Bly, Stephen and Janet. *Be Your Mate's Best Friend*. Chicago, IL: Moody Press, 1989.

Bly, Stephen and Janet. *How to Be a Good Mom*. Chicago, IL: Moody Press, 1988.

Bly, Stephen and Janet. *Welcome to the Family Seminars*. P. O. Box 157, Winchester, ID 83555.

Chapman, Gary. *Toward a Growing Marriage* (cassette tapes). Chicago, IL: Moody Press, 1979.

Chapman, Gary. *Toward a Growing Marriage Seminar*. Marriage Seminar, P. O. Box 10285, Winston-Salem, NC 27108.

Chapman, Gary. *Hope for the Separated.* Chicago. IL: Moody Press, 1982.

Dahl, Gerald. *Why Christian Marriages Are Breaking Up.* Nashville, TN: Thomas Nelson Publishers, 1979.

Dobson, Dr. James. *Emotions: Can You Trust Them?* Ventura, CA: Regal, 1980.

Fooshee, George, Jr. *You Can Be Financially Free.* Old Tappan, NJ: Revell, 1976.

Groom, Nancy. *Married Without Masks.* Colorado Springs, CO: NavPress, 1989.

LaHaye, Tim and Beverly. *The Act of Marriage.* Grand Rapids, MI: Zondervan, 1976.

Leman, Dr. Kevin. *Sex Begins in the Kitchen.* Ventura, CA: Regal Books, 1981.

Mason, Mike. *The Mystery of Marriage.* Portland, OR: Multnomah Press, 1985.

Wheat, Ed. *Sex Techniques and Sex Problems in Marriage.* Springdale, AR: Bible Believers Cassettes, 1975.

Wright, Norman. *The Pillars of Marriage.* Ventura, CA: Regal Books, 1979. ■

Janet Chester Bly is cofounder with husband, Stephen, of "Welcome to the Family" Seminars.

Janet has written and cowritten thirteen books, including *How to Be a Good Mom, Be Your Mate's Best Friend,* and *Friends Forever, The Art of Lifetime Relationships.*

She has also published hundreds of articles, short stories, devotions, and poems in numerous Christian publications.

Janet has three sons—Russell, Michael, and Aaron—and one grandson, Zachary. ■

OTHER TITLES IN THIS SERIES

Additional *CRISISPOINTS* Bible studies include:

> *Getting a Grip on Guilt* by Judith Couchman. Learn to live a life free from guilt.

> *Nobody's Perfect, So Why Do I Try to Be?* by Nancy Groom. Get over the need to do everything right.

> *So What If You've Failed?* by Penelope J. Stokes. Use your mistakes to become a more loving, godly woman.

> *When You Can't Get Along* by Gloria Chisholm. How to resolve conflict according to the Bible.

> *You're Better Than You Think!* by Madalene Harris. How to overcome shame and develop a healthy self-image.

These studies can be purchased at a Christian bookstore. Or order a catalog from NavPress, Customer Services, P. O. Box 6000, Colorado Springs, CO 80934. Or call 1-800-366-7788 for information. ■